Windows 10:

2020 Complete Beginners Guide to Learn Microsoft Windows 10 . Take Control of Your PC.

Windows 10

Copyright © 2020

All rights reserved.

ISBN: 9798616806024

CONTENTS

Introduction 6

Chapter 1 Everything you need to know before you start with new Operating system. 8

WINDOWS 10 SYSTEM REQUIREMENTS 11

UPDATE TO WINDOWS 10 12

What you will not find in other operating systems: 13

Chapter 2 Alternatives to Windows 10 15

Alternative 1 - Modern Linux Distributions 17

Alternative 2 CHROME OS 27

Alternative 3 FREEBSD 28

Alternative 4 SYLLABLE 29

Alternative 5 REACTOS 29

Alternative 6 HAIKU 30

Alternative 7 MORPHOS AND AROS 31

Alternative 8 Android-x86 31

Alternative 9 Mac OS X 32

Chapter 3 Windows History from Windows 1.0 to Windows 10 ...34

Windows 1.0 35

Windows 2.0...36

Windows / 286 2.10 and Windows / 386 2.10..............................36

Windows 3.0...37

Windows 3.1 and 3.11 37

Windows 95 38

Windows 98..38

Windows 2000 39

Windows me 39

Windows XP 39

Windows vista 40

Windows 7..40

Windows 8 40

Windows 10 41

Chapter 4 How to install Windows 10 47

The clean install of Windows 10 (version 1909) 47

How to reset Windows 10 or automatically reinstall the OS..........51

Reset Windows 10 in settings from the installed system................52

Automatic clean installation of Windows 10 using the "New Start" (Refresh Windows Tool) 53

How to reset Windows 10 if the system does not start or reset from the settings does not work 55

Windows 10 Factory Reset Errors 57

How to transfer licensed Windows 10 to another computer 59

Chapter 5 Configure Windows 10 after installation 64

    Why configure Windows 10 manually 65

Settings that need to be done after installing the OS 67

    Auto tuning system 69

    Installing Missing Drivers 71

    System update 72

    Turn off auto updates 73

    General service limitation 74

    Radical restriction of services 75

Software installation 76

Conclusion 80

I

Introduction

Radical changes to Windows 8 were perceived very differently by users. That is why Microsoft has taken such a serious approach to the new system that they have even invited enthusiasts to participate in a special Windows Insider program. Volunteers received previous versions of the new system, and Microsoft responded with criticism and worked to correct errors and shortcomings. On July 29,

Windows 10

Microsoft released a new version of its operating system - Windows 10. One of the key features of the "tens" is a voice assistant with the elements of artificial intelligence Cortana, which significantly simplifies life, performing various tasks such as scheduling meetings, searching for files and information, or table reservation in a restaurant. Unfortunately, it is not yet available in Ukraine. Windows 10 also features a new Microsoft Edge Internet browser, replacing Internet Explorer. The transition to the new Operating System is free for a year for users who have a licensed version of one of the previous operating systems - Windows 7 or Windows 8 / 8.1. In addition, with the release of Windows 10, Microsoft is moving to a new SaaS business model, in which Windows will advance as a service. This means that all updates, current security settings and services will be installed automatically.

Chapter 1 Everything you need to know before you start with new Operating system.

What's Windows?

It's no secret to anyone that the launch of Windows 10 was the last launch of the Operating System in the usual sense of Microsoft. The company decided to change the focus of activity on the development of services and will expand this particular area of activity. As soon as users install Windows 10 on their computers, their devices will begin to receive the latest updates to the operating system. For example, now there is no support for the innovative technology of augmented reality Microsoft Hololens and, as soon as the device is officially unveiled, the system will also begin to update to support this functionality.

During the first year after the release of Windows, namely until July 29, 2016, any user who owns genuine versions of Windows 7, Windows 8, and Windows 8.1 can download the Windows 10 update for free.

By the way, it is precise with the presence of Windows 8.1 in the line that the new Operating System was called Windows 10. The fact is that, in fact, Windows 8.1 is not a big update of Windows 8, but a completely different version of the OS, which was supposed to be the "nine". Therefore, such a strange collision occurred in terms of the numbering of the new Windows operating system.

New features and new features, applications and an updated interface - all this awaits the user in Windows 10. But, perhaps, the main thing is the impressions of the new OS, which can be obtained only by installing a new version of this product.

In our case, the update took place from the boxed version of Windows 7 Home Extended, which, as part of the upgrade program, turned into Windows 10 Home. It is important to note that a direct upgrade to Windows 10 Home is possible for users of Windows 7 Starter, Home Basic, Home Advanced, and Windows 8.1. Windows 10 Pro version is available for Windows 7 Professional and Ultimate, as well as Windows 8.1 Professional and Professional for students.

Installation is carried out using the application, which was released after the update and has the code name KB3035583. At some point, the "Window" symbol appeared in the lower right corner of users' computers - the logo of the new OS, which makes it possible to reserve a system update until July 29, 2016. After that, users could calmly wait for the moment when the installation files are downloaded to the computer, and the system will inform you that it is ready to upgrade. Also on the day of the release of the new OS, July 29, 2015, a special utility appeared on the Microsoft website that allows not only downloading installation files but also creating installation media.

In our case, it took about an hour to install Windows 10. During this time, the system is gradually installed on the PC, while it requires several reboots. Our system decided that it was finally ready to work after three restarts. True, we had to make another reboot already manually, since Windows 10 incorrectly set the screen resolution and did not allow us to enter the "Settings". But after the fourth reboot, the system began to work clearly, and the resolution format itself was set to "true" 1920 by 1200 pixels.

In fact, installing Windows 10 is a comprehensive software update. Since you don't have to format disks, delete old programs and reinstall them, everything that worked before will work in Windows 10. And it's really very convenient.

WINDOWS 10 SYSTEM REQUIREMENTS

Keep in mind the fact that this Operating System can be used for several types of devices - from all-in-ones to mobile phones or the Xbox One game console. If we talk about the main version for computers, then there are the following system requirements:

- A processor with a frequency of at least 1 GHz
- RAM from 1 GB (for 32 systems) and 2 GB (for 64 systems)
- 16 to 20 GB of free hard disk space
- Availability of Direct X 9 and higher

For mobile devices, the system requirements are slightly different:

- Screen with a resolution of at least 800x480
- RAM 512 MB or higher

In general, the requirements have not changed compared to the eighth version. The reason is good optimization and the absence of fundamentally new features in the system.

UPDATE TO WINDOWS 10

As mentioned earlier, the company's marketing move allows for an upgrade for users. It is available to owners of Windows 7, 8, as well as 8.1. Throughout the year from the date of release (until June 29, 2016), the update is free. Download speed depends on specific conditions, and the installation procedure itself will take about an hour. You must use the update download center or directly download the Operating System from the official Microsoft website.

The edition of Windows 10 depends on what system was previously. The installation principle is extremely simple. The edition after the update is similar to the one that was on the seven or eight. If this does not suit you, then you will have to forget about the free promotion and purchase the OS.

What you will not find in other operating systems:

An innovative approach to working under any load, which allows you to use this Operating System as if it were a universal program that is simply not simply filled with various applications, which, in turn, can be launched at the moment you need them.

The completely updated look of the Windows 10 operating system is also impossible to ignore since it has everything that you could see earlier in Windows 7 and Windows 8. Thus, it seems that you have at your disposal a new operating system, but having a very familiar appearance.

Only the "ten" can offer any user a really huge number of different kinds of editions, among which, everyone can choose for themselves exactly what he really needs.

Constant updates of the operating system also play an important role in its use, since with them you can easily notice how the Operating System actually evolves, which is getting better and better day after day.

Additional innovations of Win 10 by its developers give the program a more complete look, which in essence does not stop developing, but constantly evolves and makes the program even more popular and filled with various kinds of opportunities for work and entertainment.

A huge Operating System toolkit that will pleasantly surprise you, since such a globally filled OS that could have at its disposal a huge number of different tools: updating, restoring, scanning, cleaning, deleting, etc., had not once been in Windows.

Chapter 2 Alternatives to Windows 10

To imagine a computer world without Windows is as unrealistic as a kitchen without a stove. Starting its journey back in 1985 and having survived numerous modifications since then, this Operating System overcame a flurry of criticism, did not drown in the sea of praises, survived in fierce competition, without losing a commercial entity (even piracy did not bring it to naught). According to various sources, the share of Windows on the market today is 91.9–94.7%, the rest is shared between MacOS (6%) and Linux (3%). The experimental Operating System for enthusiasts and half-dead projects are not taken into account.

It would seem that the victory is unconditional and it makes no sense to look for something alternative? In general, yes. No matter how strange it sounds, but an ordinary user is simply obliged to associate his fate with Windows - this is guaranteed to allow you to use any acquired software and application software, write music, launch games, and process photos. Well, work, of course. Another OS is not so comfortable in any case - you will have to put up not only with the lack of a typical AO, but also with the guaranteed status of a white crow in the computer community.

Nevertheless, the need for another OS often arises, and therefore it is worthwhile to know which one is most appropriate in a particular scenario.

Alternative 1 - Modern Linux Distributions

If you remember those happy years, when few people knew which way to approach the computer, you have already heard the legends of the legendary Linux, which was invented not by the son of a rich man, but by a simple European hacker Linus Torvalds.

In these legends you were told about the super skills that you need to have to use Linux, because this operating system is for advanced users.

You may not know how to reinstall Windows 10 yourself, but everyone has heard of Linux. Despite the fact that most of us are sure that there is nothing else in the world except the usual "Winda" in the world, there is Linux. Somewhere out there. Outside this world. And this Operating System is legendary and divine.

Benefits of the Linux operating system:

1 The first thing modern Linux has ever stood out is the diversity of appearance. Perhaps that's what he bribes initially. It looks almost like Windows, but

you want to change the light view of the windows to the dark - change. The choice of options is really huge. You want to close the button to look different - please, you want all three buttons to be on the windows on the left, not on the right - tick in the right menu. There are more than 1,000 different topics for Linux. We're serious. You can make it look like Windows XP. And if you're smiling right now, it's for nothing. There are those that customize Linux to make the most of Windows or Operating System X.

2 Also Linux promises a couple of cool buns. For example, licensed Linux is free. It can be used in enterprises. It is officially free, while the license key on Windows 10 Home Edition (the simplest verse) costs about 8500 Russian rubles.

3 Linux consumes few resources, unlike Bill Gates's Window. So it's faster. And if you have an old laptop or PC, Linux will not be "capricious".

4 All applications can not be searched on the Internet, and download from the official store: quickly and for free. And much easier than

downloading from windows Store.

Mind you, we use the word "free" too often in relation to Linux.

5 And there are almost no viruses on Linux. Just a few people are interested in doing viruses on Linux. Windows is much more interesting.

6 It is hard to find on Linux the usual Vindov programs, but there are many worthy alternatives, such as LibreOffice, as a decent, quick and simple version of the usual Ward and Axel. But by great desire, Linux can still run Adobe Photoshop.

Linux flaws

1.The system is really for advanced users. They say that Linux is hard to follow on the network, but if they want to, they will find you, even when you will hack the Kremlin from the calculator. So don't be 100% safe.

2. The main drawback of Linux is a kind of illusion of simplicity. Everything seems to be simple and clear, but it is at first glance. Our first Linux Mint engineer spent two hours figuring out how to set up a second language and set up keyboard keys. He didn't make it. There was simply no Tonguetab on the menu. He ended up watching a youtube video of the manual. It turned out that the language additive function in Linux, and the change of keyboard layout lies in another menu option, which we would not have thought of in life. So it's probably going to be harder than boring Winda.

3. Another drawback, as it turned out to be a flaw in Linux - the notorious speed of Operating System download and work in the system. On 4 nuclear PCs with 8GB of RAM, the same Windovs 10 downloaded faster, and worked faster than Linux Mint Cinnamon 18. Many times faster.

4. There are a lot of Linux software, and you can get used to them.

For example, having tried LibreOffice once, we have always disliked Microsoft Word. Especially the latest versions. In addition to being easier, faster, It's a very popular free text editing and markup program. Once in its development took and invested the world's leading corporations: Oracle, Google. This was done in order to make a decent free alternative to Windows programs. And it worked.

At the same time, the notorious genius Steve Jobs took LibreOffice, remade it and "stuck" in his "Mac". LibreOffice is called OpenOffice on Macs. Only fonts and appearance were remade.

Forget about the usual progs for working with 3D models, and other programs with a narrow-profile focus, such as programs for estimators and architects. You can find decent alternatives on Linux, but that's a bad thing if they don't go or start flying when you install or start the bug. Here programmers with Linux were luckier (they are the ones who often shout about Linux as a better OS). There are a lot of code editing programs out there.

5. But despite all our trials of fate, sorry Linux, we

could not stand and ran from it that was strong. The fact that after 3 days of "persistent sex" of our brains with this OS, came across on the Internet on a video in which the presenter convinced immediately: "If you have a gaming PC, you do not need Linux. In general. Well, we ran.

Today, "Windows 10" works faster, and there are more opportunities on it.

7 of the best Linux distributions

But if you do choose Linux, we present with 7 of the best modern Linux distributions, which will fall in love with yourself at once:

1. Mint

If you've never heard of this operating system, you've lost a lot. In fact, the Linux core is even used in your smartphone. After all, Android is a kind of Linux.

This operating system is not yet able to compete with Windows, but it is not inferior in performance to it. In addition, it is free, which Linux huge advantage over the Vindows.

Why did you come up with Linux?

Many people don't understand why this operating system was created. However, the answer is obvious. This is an alternative that gives you the opportunity to try something different.

If you've been sitting on Windows all your life and then tried to switch to Linux Mint, you're probably feeling uncomfortable. This is understandable, because these are completely different operating systems.

You need to use it for a few weeks to understand what it is and for what purpose it is intended.

A weak computer is not a verdict

With the release of the 10th version of The Winds, the old computers to put it mildly were in shock. After all, their system parameters are not enough to use the operating system normally. And then comes to the rescue Linux Mint, which is less demanding to the iron of your computer. And you don't need to buy a new computer in order to use the operating system normally. The old iron is enough for the tasks quite.

2. Debian

Debian Operating System is small in size and light. It will work without problems even on weak computers. Based on Linux, this operating system has increased security requirements that guarantee protection against external attacks by attackers.

3. Manjaro

Manjaro is an offshoot of Arch Linux, a distribution that is renowned for setting everything you can for. But it has two drawbacks: a fairly high threshold of entry (it is better not to put newcomers) and "re-actuality" of software - programs are rarely thoroughly checked, and the package can go untested. The developers of Manjaro solved these problems by making a graphic installer (or rather took the Calamares project) and replacing the Arch Linux repositories with their own, where additional testing of packages takes place. As a result, updates are coming in quickly enough and already proven. There were no differences in the repositories, plus support for the custom repository (AUR) remained.

4. Ubuntu

It is cost operating system, which is in the first place among users of alternative OS. It has a user-friendly interface that can be customized so that the look looks look as similar to Windows as possible. With Ubuntu, as with other Linux-based Os, you don't have to be afraid of viruses. Pre-installed programs have everything you need to work.

5. openSUSE

UnIX-like operating system OpenSUSE has a dark green interface and is capable of working on weak computers. Has several varieties and preinstalled applications.

6. Fedora

Fedora is a Linux-like operating system, the main feature of which is working with free software.

In addition, Fedora is one of the first to receive fresh software updates that will allow you to have access to the most advanced technologies that provide an increased level of security and speed.

7. Elementary OS

Elementary OS is a quick and easy-to-learn replacement for Windows.

Developers position the system as a simple environment to work, which logically follows from the name of the OS. Elementary OS is a free operating system that is capable of running on almost any hardware. Elementary OS provides a user-friendly and up-to-date interface. The entire operating system is made in the style of minimalism. Thanks to the simplicity of the interface,

Elementary OS will understand even a newcomer to the world of Linux. All settings are intuitive, which means that it will be easier to customize the system for yourself.

If you have a weak computer or just want to get an "easy" OS, boldly install Elementary OS.

Alternative 2 CHROME OS

ChromeOS is a good replacement for Google's Windows. It can replace Windows for browsing the Internet and office work. This operating system comes preinstalled on budget devices that are known as chromebooks. In addition, Chrome OS has two versions, one that comes with laptops and free open source that can be downloaded on the internet.

ChromeOS is very lightweight and focused most on cloud technology. It's a great choice for internet surfing, browsing social networks and working with text. The system does not have traditional applications, there is only a browser in which everything works. Therefore, games and more complex work tasks can be difficult. But here you can run Android apps.

Alternative 3 FREEBSD

You can often hear that FreeBSD is Linux, but you do not have to think that FreeBSD is just another Linux distribution. Although the system has similar roots to Unix and Linux, it is a modern version of the Berkeley Software Distribution (BSD) operating system.

The system can be considered a relative of Linux, but its code can be found in various places, such as Apple's MacOS or Sony's PlayStation 4 operating system. A robust operating system primarily caters to servers, but can also be used for the desktop. By default, the system comes without desktop surroundings, but supports Gnome, KDE and Xfce. FreeBSD will be most exciting for people who care about their privacy and online security. The system is developed by TrustedBSD and is supported by companies such as McAfee, DARPA, Google, Apple and many others. We've previously looked at the differences between FreeBSD and Linux.

Alternative 4 SYLLABLE

This operating system is designed and optimized for home computers. It's based on the Linux kernel and parts of the GNU project. Syllable is another free Alternative Windows. The system is based on AtheOS and has its own browser based on WebKit. In addition, there is an email client, media player and application development environment.

This system offers a variety of OpenSource applications, such as Apache, Vim, Python. In addition, there is a server version of the system. But at the moment the system is not ready for use in production, it is simply not ready yet, although it is great for developers. A 32-bit computer with 32MB of RAM is enough to run the system. Not many systems can boast of running on such old equipment.

Alternative 5 REACTOS

If you do not want to use Linux or Unix similar systems, but you need a free windows analogue, you might be interested in ReactOS.

The project began in 1995 as a clone of Windows 95. The developers say that the purpose of the system is to allow you to remove Windows and install ReactOS instead so that the user does not notice the difference. Once reinstalled, you should be able to use your computer as well as before.

Now ReactOS is in the state of the alpha version and will be in this state for a very long time. Complicating matters is the fact that developers cannot work freely on the operating system and should try to keep up with Microsoft. But now you can run a lot of Windows apps in the system, such as Adobe Reader, Java, NetBeans IDE, and others. In total, most of the programs that work in Win work.

Alternative 6 HAIKU

Haiku is a continuation of the already closed BeOS project. This system is also free and open source. The first version was released in 2001. Since then, the system has been developing and already you can run VLC Media Player, WebPositie browser and several versions of Quake. However, the system is still in the alpha stage, and it works even worse than ReactOS.

Alternative 7 MORPHOS AND AROS

MorphOS is an interesting operating system available for PowerPC and similar devices. Of course, the probability that your Windows computer is running on a PowerPC processor is zero, but such processors can be used in older iMac, Mac Mini or Power Mac. You can run MorphOS on all of them.

AROS is a very similar system to MorphOS, but built for x86. This means that you can run it on any computer. These operating systems were designed for Amiga computers, but now you can install them on your computer and run old games and programs.

Alternative 8 Android-x86

But this is the most Android, which can be installed on an ordinary PC built on the x86 platform. They are developing this system, of course, not at Google, but the project supports all resources, including the Play Market. Those who are ready to work with the stationary version, as well as numerous applications, should carefully study this solution.

Especially if there is a need to reanimate an old laptop, and reluctance to return to the "Windows". Of course, "Android" is a specific thing and you cannot call it a full-fledged replacement for Windows, but you often need to replace an excessively monstrous product with something easy, quick and uncomplicated. And most importantly, Android is familiar to all owners of mobile gadgets.

Alternative 9 Mac OS X

Of course, it is not free and, as a rule, is purchased with a computer. Of course, I am aware of the possibility of installing MacOS on any computer, and I have also heard about the Hackintosh project, but all this is more for uncompromising fans. What drives them? Well, for example, the acquisition of an iPad or iPhone and the subsequent desire to join the Yabloko camp.

In principle, the Macintosh is very easy to use, although, like any other OS, at first it takes effort. The main disadvantages are the high cost and attachment to equipment, the lack of flexibility in use and the monstrous monetization of everything.

Overall, I repeat, without any problems, you can

forget about the settings and management difficulties - the system is very friendly and does not require special knowledge from the owner. And finally, the most important thing: almost all programs have their own versions for Macs, including games and other media content.

Chapter 3 Windows History from Windows 1.0 to Windows 10

The so-called "digital" or "computer" era, which began at the end of the last century, has turned the names of many brands into common nouns, which many to this day refer to entire families of programs or devices. For example, all copiers with the easy hands of inexperienced users turned into "photocopiers", graphic editors were generalized under the brand name "Photoshop", and any operating system was simply referred to as "Windows".

To earn such popular recognition is very difficult, and maintaining such a "monopoly" in its market segment was worth every titanic effort. For example, Microsoft has been pleasing its fans with frankly failed OS versions for more than thirty years of Windows's existence, however, at the cost of expensive marketing campaigns and attracting the best specialists to work on bugs, it continues to be the No. 1 desktop manufacturer worldwide.

But how it all began ...

Windows 1.0

Two years after the announcement, at the end of November 1985, the 16-bit Microsoft Windows 1.0 operating system was released. According to contemporaries, the result of the work of Redmond developers still could not overtake Apple's platform created at the same time in terms of usability. In fact, Windows 1.0 was an add-on for MS-DOS. It is curious that Microsoft stopped supporting the first "windows" only on December 31, 2001.

Windows 2.0

The second version of the Microsoft OS was released two years after the first, in December 1987. There were no significant innovations, as such. We can only mention the ability of windows in the system to overlap each other.

Windows / 286 2.10 and Windows / 386 2.10

Both versions were released in 1988. In connection with the release of the new Intel 80286 and Intel 80386 processors, the platforms were adapted for them. The main innovations in Windows / 286 were the availability of an extended memory driver (himem.sys), and a secure password appeared in Windows / 386. The release of these two "add-ons" was dictated by Microsoft exceeding the barrier to addressing RAM. In other words, the famous words of Gates that 640 KB is enough for everyone, ceased to be relevant.

Windows 3.0

Windows 3.0 was much more popular than its predecessors, however, it remained far from the indicators of demand for Apple's OS, which was based on the Macintosh, and the Amiga platform from Commodore. The minimum system requirements of this version of the "windows" were more than modest from the point of view of modern programs, and at that time they were standard - 384 KB of RAM and 6-7 MB free on disk. By the way, in this version, the favorite game of housewives - "Solitaire" - first appeared.

Windows 3.1 and 3.11

The first, breaking their own records of popularity, versions of the OS, which, incidentally, brought Microsoft the title of "the most innovative US company" according to Forbes magazine in 1992. Users remembered these versions by the appearance of the Sapper game and multimedia support in them.

Windows 95

In fact, Microsoft's "finest hour". This version of the operating system appeared at the end of August 1995 and quickly removing the main competitor in the person of OS / 2 from IBM from the stage, it gained unprecedented popularity. This was the last OS that came on floppy disks. Distinctive features of Windows 95 are still known - Explorer, taskbar and Start button. In addition, the novelty was the ability to instantly change the resolution of the monitor, as well as connecting plug-n-play devices. Incidentally, it was in this version that the "blue screen of death" first appeared.

Windows 98

In fact, the corrected version of Windows 95, which expanded support for USB devices. After the release of the system was delayed, a "blue screen of death" appeared.

Windows 2000

Windows NT Professional line of Windows NT. The launch took place in 1999-2000.

Windows me

Version for home use. You were in 2000, being the last operating system of the 9.x family. The system requirements were as follows - a Pentium II 300 MHz processor, 64 MB of RAM and 2 GB of disk space.

Windows XP

Again the "domesticated" version of the OS, but based on a more reliable server kernel Windows NT. Due to the fact that networking has become the world's most popular operating system, it has been released for ten years - since its release in 2001 and in 2011. In 2012, it remained the second most popular after Windows 7. The market share of this OS in 2007 reached 75%.

Windows vista

It was released in two versions: for corporate clients in 2006 and for home PCs in 2007. Due to increased system requirements, the limited rights protection mechanism (DRM) was not popular among users. Great support and multimedia support.

Windows 7

The second most popular OS from Microsoft after Windows XP. This is the most requested operating system. Unlike Vista in this release, developers are focused on improving reliability and compatibility. Nevertheless, despite the support for multi-touch, the system is desktop and annual for installation on tablets, which continue to gain popularity among users.

Windows 8

In February 2012, public testing of the new OS,

Windows 8, was launched. The main innovation was the ability to install on ARM tablets and optimize for finger control. In the G8, the built-in virtual store Windows Store is a kind of analog of the App Store and Android Market. The clock frequency of 1 GHz, at least 1 GB of RAM and 16-20 GB of hard disk space. Start Button. As a result, the new product was in fairly moderate demand and could not throw Windows 7 from the position of leader.

Windows 10

Most users do not get detailed and evaluating operating systems from the first, often superficial (but often correct) sensations that combine the "dozens" of Microsoft for inconclusive Windows 8. Indeed, even the first description made it clear that the new version of the OS has clearer outlines.

Unlike its predecessors, Windows 10 was fully functional for hybrid laptops with touch screens or dancing with a tambourine around the Start button. Key innovations of the system: Cortana's voice assistant, OS support on any device (smartphones, tablets, PCs, Xbox, etc.), the ability to create multiple desktops and convenient interactions, the brand new Edge browser, which replaced Internet

Explorer.

Features of OS Windows 10

By the numerous requests of users, the Start button and all the usual conveniences of working with the desktop Desktop have been returned. Some other features that were in the very first versions of Windows were returned, and then somehow disappeared.

• Truly multi-window work available. You can display several applications on the screen at the same time and switch flexibly.

• When connecting multiple monitors, applications can be displayed on separate displays - these are real Windows, the concept of working in parallel in several applications.

• All new applications are fully adapted to any type of device. After purchasing the program, it will automatically work on all computers owned by the user: on the desktop, tablet, and smartphone running Windows 10.

Windows 10

• A new Edge browser was developed to replace I.E. It seems that the Microsoft developers decided to take advantage of the best finds of the creators of Firefox and Chrome. Extensions from Mazila and Chrome can be integrated into the new browser from Microsoft.

As a certain inconvenience for residents of the CIS can be called the lack of the usual Windows Media Center and the ability to play DVDs. Video in this format in the West has long been considered obsolete, but we still use it. Inactive development, the Cortana voice control system. Soon, the keyboard and mouse will be anachronisms.

Windows 10 issues

Many, if not most users do not like the system of forced download and installation of Windows 10 updates. The bottom line is that as usual with Microsoft, bugs in innovations are not uncommon, and after automatic updates, Windows 10 starts to "fail". You cannot disable automatic updates. In addition, unceremonious interference in the privacy of users. Windows 10, as stated, will collect information about the use of the device and, without the permission of the owner, send it to Microsoft for analysis and research. That's when the user recalls that Microsoft is an American corporation, the thought immediately arises of the CIA, NSA, and Snowden. There is no guarantee that Microsoft will not merge users' personal data into US intelligence agencies. As often happened, including with the American social network Facebook.

Pros and Benefits of Windows 10

In terms of consumer experience, Windows 10 is truly a new level of comfort. You could even say - this is the future of information technology. Additional bonuses stem from the rather aggressive promotion of OS Windows 10 to the market.

- For owners of Windows 8 and Windows 7, upgrading to Windows 10 is free.

- And that's not all, upgrading to Windows 10 is available even to owners of unlicensed pirated copies of Windows 7 and Windows 8. True, this will not be licensed Windows 10, the system will remain illegal, although it will be updated.

Aggressive marketing and the imposition of the transition to a new operating system eventually resulted in the gradual cessation of support for all older versions of Windows, including those so beloved by users of Windows XP and Windows 7. True, over time, under pressure from public opinion, Microsoft announced the resumption support for Windows XP and Windows 7. It really can be called a significant victory of democracy over omnipotent transnational corporations. Another big and fat plus is that the MS Office suite of office programs is now included in the basic Windows 10 distribution free of charge, and there is no need to buy Word separately for a lot of money.

The tradition of Windows 8 in creating a comfortable working environment for dynamic users continues.

• Connecting the office to cloud storage with automatic data storage.

• Convenient conditions for collaborating on documents remotely.

• Automatic adaptation of applications to any type of device.

OS Windows 10 and actually turned out to be very convenient and functional. In fact, the widespread popularization and distribution of Windows 10 is only hindered by the relatively high cost of Windows devices and license fees for most of the necessary applications.

Chapter 4 How to install Windows 10.

The clean install of Windows 10 (version 1909)

The best way to upgrade to Windows 10 November 2019 Update without any problems is to perform a clean installation. Let's see why this is actually the case, and how to perform a clean installation of Windows 10 version 1909.

The Windows 10 November 2019 Update is now available for download and installation on November 12, 2019. If you want to avoid potential problems, it is best to perform a clean installation of the system.

Although updating using Windows Update is the easiest way to install version 1909, there is a chance that you will encounter problems and errors that result from incompatible software and drivers, configuration problems, etc. A clean installation of the system minimizes the risk run into problems, because in this case all data is deleted on the hard drive and a new copy of Windows 10 November 2019 Update is installed.

In addition, if you use one installation for a long time, then a clean installation of Windows 10 can improve performance, boot time, memory consumption and fix many existing problems.

To create a bootable drive, it is recommended to use the official Microsoft tool - Media Creation Tool.

How to perform a clean install of Windows 10 (version 1909)

After creating a bootable USB drive, you can proceed with a clean installation of Windows 10:

- Insert the Windows 10 bootable drive and start the PC.
- Press any key to start the installation process.
- Click "Next".
- Click the "Install" button.
- On the "Activate Windows" screen, click the "I do not have a product key" link if you reinstall the system (after installation, Windows 10 will automatically re-activate).

Windows 10

- Select the operating system you want to install and click the "Next" button.

- Check the box "I accept the terms of the license" after reading the license agreement. and click the "Next" button.

- Select the installation type "Custom: Windows installation only (for advanced users)".

- On the "Where do you want to install Windows?" Screen select the partition on your hard drive or SSD where you want to install Windows 10, and click the "Uninstall" button. Typically, installation is performed on "Disk 0".

- Select "Unallocated disk space 0" to install Windows 10 and click "Next".

- Wait until the installation of Windows 10. The computer will restart several times.

- Select your region on the first page of the preset wizard after completing the installation procedure and click "Yes".

- Select a keyboard layout and click "Yes".

- If you do not need to configure a second layout, click the Skip button.

- If your device uses a wired Ethernet connection, then your computer will automatically connect to the network. If you use a wireless connection, then you will have to configure it manually by entering Wi-Fi network data.

- On the "Select a setup method" screen, select the "Configure for personal use" option and click the "Next" button.

- Enter the email / phone number of your Microsoft account or Skype account. You can also select "Offline account" if you do not want to create a Microsoft account.

- Set up your account.

- Set a password.

- And configure additional security settings (security questions).

- Select the privacy options that suit you best and click the "Accept" button.

- Wait for the account setup to complete. This may take several minutes.

After installation, check for the latest cumulative updates through Windows Update. To check and install, go to Settings> Update and Security and click Check for Updates.

Tip. To quickly find out the version number of Windows 10, enter "winver" in the search box, press Enter, and you will see a dialog box with information about the current version of the OS.

How to reset Windows 10 or automatically reinstall the OS

This guide contains instructions on how to reset Windows 10 to factory settings, perform a reset, rollback to its original state, or, otherwise, automatically reinstall Windows 10 on a computer or laptop. It has become easier to do this than in Windows 7 and even in 8, due to the fact that the way the image is stored for the reset in the system has changed and in most cases, you do not need a disk or flash drive in order to perform the described procedure. If for some reason all of the above fails, you can simply perform a clean install of Windows 10.

Resetting Windows 10 to its original state can come in handy in cases where the system began to work incorrectly or does not even start, and you cannot restore using another method. At the same time, reinstalling the OS in this way is possible with saving your personal files (but without saving programs

Update: in the latest versions of Windows 10 there is an additional way to reset the system with the removal of all the programs preinstalled by the manufacturer of the computer or laptop - Automatic clean installation of Windows 10.

Reset Windows 10 in settings from the installed system

The easiest way to reset Windows 10 is to assume that the system starts on your computer. If so, then a few simple steps allow you to perform an automatic reinstall.

1. Go to Settings (via start and gear icon or Win + I keys) - Update and Security - Recovery.

2. In the "Restore Computer" section, click "Start." Note: if during recovery you are informed that there are no necessary files, use the method from the next section of this instruction. Also, an error may appear at this stage: Unable to find a recovery environment.

3. You will be asked to either save your personal files or delete them. Select an option.

4. If you select the option to delete files, it will also offer either "Just delete files" or "Completely erase the disk." I recommend the first option unless you give the computer or laptop to another person. The second option deletes files without the possibility of their recovery and takes longer.

5. In the "Everything is ready to return this computer to its original state" window, click "Reset".

After that, the process of automatic reinstallation of the system will begin, the computer will restart (possibly several times), and after the reset, you will get a clean Windows 10. If you selected "Save personal files", the Windows.an old folder containing the files will also be on the system drive old system (user folders and desktop contents may come in handy there).

Automatic clean installation of Windows 10 using the "New Start" (Refresh Windows Tool)

In the latest versions of Windows 10, a new function

appeared in the recovery options - "New Startup" (formerly called the Refresh Windows Tool), which allows you to perform an automatic clean install or reinstall of Windows 10 with saving files but also removing the manufacturer's preinstalled programs. Its use allows you to perform a reset when the first method does not work and reports errors.

1. In the recovery options, at the bottom in the Advanced recovery options section, click on Find out how to start over from a clean installation of Windows.

2. You will be prompted to go to the corresponding page of the Windows 10 Security Center, click Yes.

3. Click the "Get Started" button in the "New Startup" section.

4. Familiarize yourself with what exactly is the Start Again function and, if you agree, click Next.

5. Wait until the reset of Windows 10 to the factory settings is completed.

Upon completion of the process (which may take a long time and depends on the computer's performance, the selected parameters and the amount of personal data when saving), you will receive a fully re-installed and functional Windows 10. After logging in, I also recommend that you press Win + R, enter cleanmgr, press Enter, and then click on the "Clear system files" button.

With a high probability, when you clean the hard disk, you can delete up to 20 GB of data remaining after the system reinstallation process.

How to reset Windows 10 if the system does not start or reset from the settings does not work

In cases where Windows 10 does not start or the reset does not work in the settings, you can try using the manufacturer's tools or with the recovery environment.

If Windows 10 does not start, but shows a blue screen with an error, then clicking on the item "Advanced options", you can get into the recovery environment. If the system starts, but you cannot reset the OS, go to Settings - Update and Security and click the "Restart Now" button in the "Special boot options" section.

After the reboot, go to the "Troubleshooting" section and then click on the item "Restore the computer to its original state."

Further, as well as in the first method described, you can:

1. Save or delete personal files. If you select "Delete" it will also be offered either to completely clean the disk without the possibility of their recovery, or a simple removal. Usually (if you don't give the laptop away to someone), it's best to use simple removal.

2. In the window for selecting the target operating system, select Windows 10.

3. In the "Restore Computer" window, see what will be done - uninstalling programs, resetting to default values and automatically reinstalling Windows 10 Click "Reset".

After that, the process of resetting the system to its initial state, during which the computer can restart, will begin.

If licensed Windows 10 was pre installed on your device at the time of purchase, then the easiest way to reset it to the factory settings is to use certain keys when you turn on your laptop or computer.

Windows 10 Factory Reset Errors

The first and simplest methods, if you encounter problems when resetting Windows 10 to the factory settings, consist of the following steps:

• Ensure that there is sufficient free space on the system partition of the drive (on drive C). Ideally, 10 GB or more.

• Remove all third-party antiviruses and other protection programs before starting recovery.

If, when you try to reset Windows 10 after a reboot, you see the message "There is a problem returning the PC to its original state. The change has not been made, "this usually indicates problems with the files necessary for recovery (for example, if you did something with the WinSxS folder, from which the files are reset). You can try checking and restoring the integrity of Windows 10 system files, but more often you have to do a clean installation of Windows 10 (however, you can also save personal data).

The second variant of the error is that you are asked to insert a recovery disk or installation drive. Then a solution appeared with the function Start again, described in the second section of this manual. Also in this situation, you can make a bootable USB flash drive with Windows 10 (on the current computer or on another one, if this does not start) or a Windows 10 recovery disk with the inclusion of system files. And use it as the required drive. Use the version of Windows 10 with the same bit depth that is installed on the computer.

Another option in the case of the requirement to provide a drive with files is to register your own image for system recovery (for this the OS should work, actions are performed in it). I have not tested this method, but they write that it works (but only for the second case with an error):

1. You need to download the ISO image of Windows 10 (the second method in the instructions here).

2. Mount it and copy the install.wim file from the sources folder to the previously created ResetRecoveryImage folder on a separate partition or computer disk (not the system one).

3. At the command prompt, on behalf of the administrator, use the reagentc / setosimage / path "D: \ ResetRecoveryImage" / index 1 command (here D stands as a separate section, you may have a different letter) to register the recovery image.

After that, try to restart the system reset. By the way, for the future, you can recommend making your own backup of Windows 10, which can greatly simplify the process of rolling back the OS to a previous state.

How to transfer licensed Windows 10 to another computer

If you purchased the Licensed Version of Windows 10 and after that decided to change your personal computer, you will not want to buy a license again. Now we will tell you what you need in order to transfer the license from one computer to another.

Deactivate your old PC instead of buying a new license

Windows licenses are expensive. Microsoft's official key price, from $ 100 to $ 200, can be compared to the price of a terabyte solid-state drive, 16 GB of RAM or a motherboard. And buying cheap keys from dubious websites is not a good idea. Therefore, paying for the next license when you get rid of the old computer in favor of the new one is not a very interesting idea. But the good news is that you can deactivate a PC that you will no longer use and transfer the license to a new one.

Using the slmgr command, this is quite simple, but there are some limitations to keep in mind. This will not work with OEM keys that ship with pre-built computers. Manufacturers integrate them into the equipment they come with and cannot be transferred to a new device. And if slmgr can deactivate any key purchased at retail separately, it can only activate a key that matches the installed OS.

Keys from Windows 7 and 8 can activate Windows 10, but only through the standard activation process, and not through slmgr. Also, with its help it will not be possible to enter the key from Pro in the Home edition system. To simplify the situation, transfer the key from Windows 10 Home to Windows 10 Home, and the key from Windows 10 Pro to the key from Windows 10 Pro. Otherwise, you have to make additional body movements.

How to deactivate an old PC

Before you begin, be sure to save the key. If you have a box or digital check, take it there. In other cases, there are ways to restore the key from an old PC, for example, the Nirsoft Produkey program.

To deactivate a PC, you need to open the input line with administrator capabilities. It is not enough just to run it from under the administrator account. You need to click the "Start" button, type cmd in the input field, and then click on the "Run as administrator" menu item.

In the input line that appears, run the following command, after which you will need to restart the computer:

slmgr.vbs / upk

If you plan to sell or give away your PC, it would be nice to clean your key from the registry. This is not necessary for deactivation, but it is desirable to protect the key.

Write the following on the command line:

slmgr.vbs / cpky

If successful, your old PC will be deactivated. You can use Windows, but it will no longer be activated, and some features will stop working - for example, personalizing the desktop. Everything will be the same as after installing Windows without a product key. To activate Windows, you can buy a new key and enter it, or buy it in the Windows Store.

How to activate a new PC

To activate using slmgr, open a command prompt with administrator rights and run the following command:

slmgr.vbs / ipk ##### - ##### - ##### - ##### - ##### Where instead of gratings, enter the key.

If you try to enter a key that has not been deactivated on another PC, then at first everything will look as if the activation worked. But in the end, it will stop working, and you will receive messages about the need to update the license.

I repeat that this will work only if the key matches the version of the OS you are using. If you have a key to Windows 10 Pro and Windows 10 Home is installed, you will receive an error message.

If you try to enter a key for Windows 7 or 8, you will receive an invalid key message.

In such cases, it is best to open "Settings", select "Activate Windows", and enter the key manually.

If you use the key for Pro and activate a copy of Windows 10 Home, it will upgrade to Pro automatically.

Note that the key for Windows can be used only for one installed copy of the OS. If you want to leave the old computer while assembling a new one, you will need a second license. But if you plan to get rid of it, then save money and transfer the existing license.

Chapter 5 Configure Windows 10 after installation

The Windows 10 operating system is trying to do everything itself: from installing drivers to optimizing applications. It turns out this is good for her, but if you leave all the important processes to the conscience of the operating system, you will soon find a bunch of obscure applications and services that will periodically launch, self-update and eat up all the resources of your computer. If you want to configure Windows 10 so that your computer does not have to share performance with incomprehensible services, while leaving all the useful things that the system can give you, you will have to combine the automatic installation with the manual one. This is not so easy to do, because Windows 10 practically does not tolerate interference in its processes, but if you follow all the instructions below exactly, you will not have problems with the configuration. And if you encounter some of the possible errors associated with installing and configuring the system, we will help you to completely eliminate them.

Why configure Windows 10 manually

One of the main prides of Windows 10 is the complete automation of everything that can be done, including tuning and optimizing the operating system itself. The idealized version of preparing Windows 10 for use, as Microsoft sees it, is extremely simple:

1. You are installing Windows 10.

2. The system starts up, downloads all drivers and updates itself, configures itself and restarts.

3. Windows 10 is ready to go.

In principle, this scheme works quite well, at least in most cases. And if you have a relatively good computer and you don't feel any discomfort after automatically setting up Windows 10, you can leave it as it is.

Now, let's list the disadvantages of automatic configuration:

• Microsoft is full of low-quality programs and games that need to be promoted somehow - some of them will be installed automatically on your computer;

• Microsoft wants you to pay or watch ads, but better all at once;

• automatic configuration of Windows 10 does not take into account outdated and weak hardware;

• Windows 10 is the most spying operating system in history, and it collects information from the resources of your computer;

• a huge number of secondary services that run in the background and eat RAM;

• automatic system updates that may catch you by surprise;

• application updates, service updates and updating everything in order to eat as much resources and traffic as possible;

• far from everything is working perfectly and failures are possible, and the system will not show.

Roughly speaking, without manual configuration, the computer will be used not only by you, but also by completely unnecessary services that fully fit the definition of viruses.

At the same time, Windows 10 is a surprisingly good and very productive system that really does a lot of good in automatic mode. If you want to cut out all the imposed garbage and save all the good that Windows 10 can give you, without turning the system along the way into a log, you will have to spend a little time and do manual tuning. It will take you two hours, but at the exit you will get the best system of all available, also free.

Settings that need to be done after installing the OS

As mentioned above, setting up Windows 10 is time-consuming and will take much longer than with previous versions. The main task will be to limit the amount of loaded junk, while allowing everything else to be installed, and then wipe and disable everything that could not be prevented.

The sequence of items is very important, try not to disturb the order and restart the computer after each step.

Store activation and restriction

The main task of this stage is to limit the store through a firewall, Windows activation can be performed at the very end of the configuration, but it's better now.

If your computer is already connected to the Internet, soon disconnect.

After connecting to the Internet, a mass download of drivers, updates and applications will begin. Let's prevent unnecessary applications from loading.

1. Open the "Start" menu, find "Shop" there and launch it.

2. Click on the button with the profile image at the top of the window that opens and select "Settings".

3. Uncheck the box for automatic application updates.

4. Now find the control panel through the search and open it.

5. Go to the system and security category.

6. Open "Allow application interaction through the Windows Firewall."

7. Click "Change settings", find "Shop" in the list and deprive it of all the checkmarks. After confirm the changes.

8. Now it is desirable to activate Windows. It is best to use a KMS activator. If you have not prepared the activator in advance, download it from another device, since it is advisable to make the first Internet connection with Windows 10 already activated.

9. Restart your computer.

Auto tuning system

Now it's worth letting Windows configure itself. This is the key point on which the Internet turns on.

1. At the previous stage, we limited the Microsoft store, but on some versions of Windows 10 this may not help (very rare cases). Launch the store again,

click on the user button and open "Downloads and Updates".

2. Drag the window down so that it does not bother you. Throughout the current phase, periodically look at the store window. If the download icon appears (marked in green on the screenshot), click "Stop All" and go through the crosses on all applications from the download queue. The necessary applications and important updates are not here.

3. Now it is very desirable to connect all devices to your computer: printer, joystick, and so on. If you use several screens, connect everything, press the "Win + P" key combination and select the "Expand" mode (it is it, change it after reboot).

4. The time has come to connect to the Internet. Windows 10 should do this without drivers, but if you have problems, install the driver for the network card or Wi-Fi module (download only from the manufacturer's website). More about manual driver installation is described in the next step. Now you only need to connect the Internet.

5. Now the mass download, installation and optimization will begin. Do not try to do anything with the computer: the system needs all possible resources. Windows will not notify you of the end of

the process - you have to guess for yourself. Your guideline will be the moment you install the driver for the video card: the correct screen resolution will be set. After that, wait another 30 minutes and restart the computer. If the resolution does not change even after an hour and a half or the system itself informs of completion, restart the computer.

Installing Missing Drivers

As mentioned above, Windows 10 auto-tuning may fail, which is especially true in the case of installing drivers on outdated hardware, which is not taken into account. Even if it seems to you that all the drivers are in place, it is better to check it yourself.

1. Open the control panel and expand the "Hardware and Sound" category.

2. Go to the "Device Manager".

3. Now you need to find all the devices with a yellow triangle on the icon, they will be visible immediately. If this is found, right-click on it and select "Update Driver."

4. Select automatic search. Then the system will tell

you everything.

5. If it doesn't help, which is very likely, right-click on the device again and go to its properties.

6. In the "General" tab there will be all the information that the system can learn about this equipment. Based on this data, you need to find on the Internet, download and install the missing driver yourself. If the manufacturer is indicated, first go to his website and look there. Drivers should be downloaded only from official sites.

System update

There are a lot of variations of Windows 10, tailored for different hardware and bit depth, but during installation, a universal version of the system is installed to minimize the size of the image. Windows 10 has an update center that automatically updates the system to the current version and changes the variation of Windows to the most compatible one. Updating the version is not interesting to us: the changes are minimal, completely invisible and not always useful. But optimization is very important.

As in the case of the second launch, this stage can take a lot of time.

1. Open the Start menu and go to options.

2. Select the "Update and Security" section.

3. Click "Check for Updates", wait a lot of time and restart the computer when it's over.

If nothing was found, then the system has already managed to update itself.

Maximum Performance

The automatic configuration of Windows 10 has already ended, and now it's time to clean out everything that is unnecessary so that the built-in services no longer bother you, and the system could work at full capacity and not share computer resources with parasitic processes.

Turn off auto updates

Start by disabling system auto-updates. Updates for Windows 10 come out very often and do not contain anything useful for ordinary users. But then they can start independently at the most inopportune moment, which puts pressure on the performance of your computer. And after you want to quickly reboot, you will suddenly have to wait half an hour until the updates are accepted.

You can still update the system, as described in the previous step, just now you will control this process.

1. Through the search, go to "gpedit.msc".

2. Follow the path "Computer Configuration / Administrative Templates / Windows Components" and click on "Windows Update".

3. Open "Configure Automatic Updates."

4. Check "Disable" and confirm the changes. You do not need to reboot yet.

General service limitation

As you probably know, Windows 10 is actively spying on its users. But you don't need to worry about your personal data: they are uninteresting to Microsoft. You need to worry about the resources of your computer that are spent on this espionage.

In order not to waste time digging around the

corners of your system, we will use the Destroy Windows Spying program, which will not only protect your computer from espionage, but also remove all the associated threats to the performance of your computer.

1. Download Destroy Windows Spying on the Internet and run it (this program is free). Do not rush to press the big button. Go to the "Settings" tab, enable professional mode and uncheck "Disable Windows Defender". Optionally, you can remove metro applications - these are Microsoft obsessive programs that are useful in theory but never used in practice. Some metro applications cannot be returned.

2. Return to the main tab and click on the big button. At the end of the process, be sure to restart the computer, even if you plan to use ShutUp10 described below.

Radical restriction of services

Destroy Windows 10 Spying kills only the most unpleasant processes, but much remains untouched. If you are determined to be sterile, you can perform finer cleaning of services using ShutUp10.

1. Download ShutUp10 on the Internet and run it (this is a free program). By clicking on one of the items (on the inscription), you will receive a detailed description of the service. Then choose you. Green - will be disabled, red - will remain. When you mark everything you want, close the application and restart the computer.

2. If you are too lazy to choose, expand the options and select "Apply all recommended and partially recommended settings." There will be no serious consequences, and all changes can be rolled back.

Software installation

Windows 10 is almost ready to work, it remains only to clean up the remaining garbage and heal registry errors. You can do this now, but better after you install everything you need, as new errors and garbage may appear.

Install programs and games, configure your browser and do whatever you are used to. Regarding the required software, Windows 10 has the same requirements as previous versions, with a few exceptions.

Here are the programs that are already embedded and you do not need to install them:

• archiver;

• emulator of images;

• DirectX or its updates;

• antivirus (if you are not very good at navigating the Internet, it is better to neglect our advice and still install a third-party antivirus).

If you doubt the set of necessary software, here is an exhaustive list of programs that you may need in the future:

• third-party browser (best Google Chrome or Mozilla Firefox);

• Microsoft Office (Word, Excel and PowerPoint);

• Adobe Acrobat;

• players for music and video (we recommend AIMP for music and KMPlayer for video);

• GIF Viever or another third-party program for viewing gif files;

• Skype;

• Steam;

• Ccleaner (it will be written about below);

• translator (for example, PROMT);

• antivirus (installing it on Windows 10 is rarely useful, but this is a very controversial issue - if you decide, we recommend Avast).

In the end, do not forget to restart the computer.

Ccleaner

After installing the programs and updates, a decent amount of registry errors and temporary files, which are also called junk files, should accumulate on your computer.

1. Download, install and run Ccleaner. On the "Cleanup" tab in the Windows section, check off all items except "Network Passwords", "Shortcuts in the Start menu", "Shortcuts on the desktop" and the entire "Other" group. If you have configured MIcrosoft Edge and plan to use it, do not mark its group. Do not rush to start cleaning.

2. Go to the "Applications" section and uncheck all the checkboxes there. Now click "Clear."

3. Open the "Registry" tab and click "Search for problems."

4. When the analysis is completed, click "Correct Selected ...".

5. Backups are best kept.

6. Now click "Fix selected."

7. Go to the service tab. In the "Uninstall programs" section, you can erase all the optional applications that managed to slip through during the system update. With regular methods, you will not succeed.

8. Go to the "Startup" section. In the internal tab of Windows, select all the items and click "Turn off".

9. Go to the internal tab "Scheduled Tasks" and repeat the previous step. After restart your computer.

It is advisable to leave the Cceaner program on the computer and check the system for registry errors every few months.

Conclusion

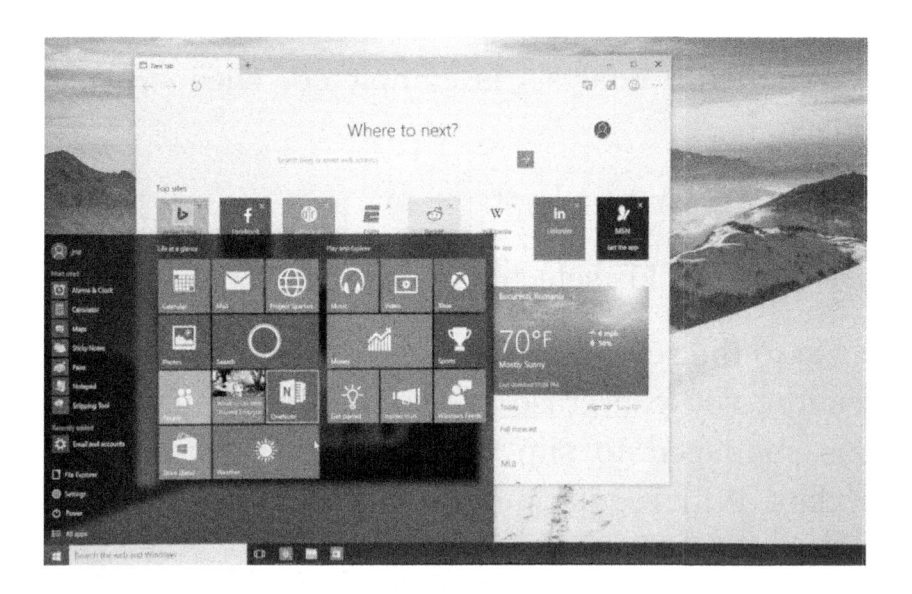

One book did not contain all the important things you need to know about Windows 10. Here I touched on the main points from which you need to start. Soon the second part of this book will be published where we will talk in detail about those things that will be useful to you. In the second part of the book you will learn:

Major changes November Update

Managing Programs, Applications and

Work on the internet

Music, Photos, and Films

How to protect your computer and personal information

Cortana tips & tricks

Tips & Tricks

Troubleshooting

And so much more.

I hope, that you really enjoyed reading my book.

Thanks for buying the book anyway!

Printed in Great Britain
by Amazon